Science and Technology

Crime-fighting Devices

Robert Snedden

Raintree

www.raintreepublishers.co.uk
Visit our website to find out more information about Raintree books.

To order:
☎ Phone 0845 6044371
📠 Fax +44 (0) 1865 312263
📧 Email myorders@raintreepublishers.co.uk

Customers from outside the UK please telephone +44 1865 312262

Edited by Andrew Farrow, Adam Miller, and Diyan Leake
Designed by Victoria Allen
Original illustrations © Capstone Global Library Ltd 2011
Illustrated by Oxford Designers and Illustrators
Picture research by Elizabeth Alexander
Originated by Capstone Global Library Ltd
Printed and bound in China by CTPS

ISBN 978 1 406 22843 4 (hardback)
15 14 13 12 11
10 9 8 7 6 5 4 3 2 1

ISBN 978 1 406 22853 3 (paperback)
16 15 14 13 12
10 9 8 7 6 5 4 3 2 1

British Library Cataloguing in Publication Data
Snedden, Robert.
  Science and technology: crime-fighting devices. -- (Sci-hi)
  364.4-dc22
A full catalogue record for this book is available from the British Library.

Acknowledgements
The author and publishers are grateful to the following for permission to reproduce copyright material: Alamy pp. **7** left, **7** right (© by Ian Miles-Flashpoint Pictures), **21** (© Chris Deeney), **26** (© Les Polders), **37** (© JoeFox); Brain Fingerprinting Laboratories, Inc. p. **41**; Corbis pp. 4 (© George Steinmetz), **6**, **31** (© Image Source), **24** (© Luis Carbayo/epa), **27** (© Chad Hunt), **34** (© Surapan Boonthanom/Reuters), **36** (© Michael Reynolds/epa); Getty Images pp. **13** (Alan Thornton), **25** (John Kirk-Anderson); Photolibrary pp. **33**, **35**; Press Association Images pp. **38** (A3471 Boris Roessler/DPA), **39** (Scott Heppell/PA Archive); Rex Features p. **20** (Fraser Spratt); Science Photo Library pp. **10** (Gustoimages), **11** (Sandia National Laboratories), **28** (Maura Fermariello); Shutterstock **contents page** top (© Kodda) **contents page** bottom (© Gina Sanders), pp. **5** (© SVLuma), **12** (© Kodda), **18** (© Paul Drabot), **19** (© Kletr), **22** (© knotsmaster), **32** (© Gina Sanders), **all background and design features**.

Main cover photograph of a taser stun gun reproduced with permission of Alamy (© Howard Sayer); inset cover photograph of fingerprint reproduced with permission of shutterstock (© melki76).

The publisher would like to thank literary consultant Nancy Harris and content consultant Suzy Gazlay for their assistance in the preparation of this book.

Every effort has been made to contact copyright holders of material reproduced in this book. Any omissions will be rectified in subsequent printings if notice is given to the publisher.

Disclaimer

Contents

Why do governments use CCTV?

Turn to page 12 to find out!

What is predictive analytics?

Find out on page 32!

Some words are shown in bold, **like this**. These words are explained in the glossary. You will find important information and definitions underlined, <u>like this</u>.

ONE STEP AHEAD

Law enforcement agencies such as police forces must be ready to respond quickly to the threat of crime. There are many ways in which science and technology can help them do this.

A person can be **identified** (found out) from a drop of blood or a single hair. Remote-controlled aircraft watch from above, and clever computer programs might even pinpoint crimes before they are committed.

The police can keep an eye on events and spot trouble quickly from command centres like this one.

Combating crime

People who commit crimes don't want to be caught. They are always trying to find different ways to "get away with it". In many ways the police and **security services** are always trying to keep one step ahead of criminals.

Cyber-crime

Computer crime, or cyber-crime, can involve cracking codes and passwords to break into computer systems. People who do this are called hackers. The police need to have computer skills, too, so they can combat this type of crime. Not all computer hackers are criminals. Many use their talents to help the police. They show them where there might be weaknesses in computer security, for example.

Secret skills

For some tasks, the police and security services carefully guard the systems they use and the skills they have. One such task is in dealing with explosive devices. The people who do this are called bomb disposal experts. They keep the methods they use to make bombs safe a secret. Because of this, **terrorists** and criminals aren't sure what to do to make their bombs more likely to succeed.

Mobile patrols can be sent swiftly to the scene of a crime.

CRIME PREVENTION

A lot of crime fighting involves preventing crime from happening in the first place. Protecting buildings using warning systems such as **intruder**, or burglar alarms can help to do this. Another way to prevent theft is to mark **property** (belongings) so that they can be readily identified. Thieves are put off from stealing items that they can't get rid of easily.

Make sure you have a good, sturdy lock for your bike – and don't forget to use it.

BRIGHT IDEA: SIMPLE STEPS

There are a number of simple steps you can take to protect yourself and your belongings. For example, you should keep valuable objects such as phones and mp3 players safely out of sight. Never leave any of your property unattended in a public place. Make sure doors and windows are closed and locked at night or when you leave the house. That's a very clever idea!

Security sprays

Researchers have developed sprays that contain millions of tiny particles that are too small to be seen with the naked eye. Each particle carries a code. The code is logged in a police **database** (collection of information). No two particle sprays have the same code. The spray is applied to property and evaporates leaving the particles invisibly behind. Details of the owner of the property are also logged in the police database. If the property is stolen, it can be identified by examining the particles through a microscope.

Another type of spray contains a number of different chemicals. As with the particle spray, no two sprays have exactly the same combination of chemicals. A system can be set up to spray the chemical mixture on intruders who enter a building. The spray will remain invisibly on their skin for weeks. It will glow brightly if ultraviolet light is shone on it. If the police find someone with the spray on their skin or clothes, they can prove that they were at the scene of a crime by identifying the chemical combination of the spray.

The security spray on this shoe shows up clearly in ultraviolet light (left). Under ordinary light (right) it is invisible.

Intruder alert

Intruder, or burglar, alarms are used to protect homes and other buildings. They are used to send out an alert if an intruder attempts to break in. There are several different kinds of alarms.

Circuit breakers

One of the most basic types of alarm works like a switch in an **electric circuit**. A switch is a type of circuit breaker. It breaks the flow of electricity around the circuit. For example, a light can be turned on and off by flicking a switch. In the same way, a window or a door can be wired to act like a switch that activates a burglar alarm. One of the easiest ways of doing this is to have a small button in the frame of the door or window. When the door is opened, the button is released, triggering the alarm. These circuit breaker systems are best for stopping people getting in to a building.

Infrared sensors

A warm object, such as a person, gives off **infrared** (heat) radiation. Infrared **sensors** in a room are sensitive enough to detect the increase in heat if a person enters. Because infrared light beams are invisible, they can also be used like "tripwires". Rays of infrared light are beamed across the room. If someone moving around the room breaks one of these beams, an alarm is sounded.

Motion sensors

A criminal may find ways to get past a circuit breaker alarm, but there are ways to detect an intruder moving inside a building. <u>Motion sensors are devices that detect movement</u>. Some motion sensors work by sending out bursts of **microwaves** (invisible energy waves). These are reflected back to the sensor from the objects in the room. Anybody moving in the room will interfere with the reflections. These changes will be detected by the sensor, which will set off an alarm.

Sensor

Microwave signal

Sensor

Microwave signal bounces from moving person

Moving person

A motion sensor in a room uses invisible microwaves to pick up the movements of an intruder.

Airport security

The police take the threat of a terrorist attack very seriously indeed. Security is very tight at airports in particular. <u>Taking control of an aircraft by force is called hijacking</u>. If anything happens to an aircraft when it is in the air there is very little that anyone on the ground can do to help. X-ray machines, metal detectors, and electronic explosive "sniffers" are all used to prevent dangerous items being taken on board an aircraft.

X-ray machines

As you pass through the departure area of an airport, an X-ray machine examines any bags you have. <u>X-rays are high-energy beams that can pass through anything that isn't a metal, or that contains metals</u>. (The calcium in bones is metallic, which is why bones show up in X-rays.) The X-rays help security staff see what's inside every bag. Before baggage goes into the hold of an aircraft it will be checked for suspicious items. Sometimes a lorry carrying a mobile X-ray system is used to scan a whole lorryload of baggage.

An X-ray machine reveals the contents of this case.

Metal detectors

You will walk through a metal detector while your belongings go through the X-ray machine. The metal detector works by using an **electromagnet**, a type of magnet produced by a flow of electric current. The current is switched on and off very rapidly. This sends pulses of magnetic force from one side of the detector to the other. If a metal object, such as a knife, is present it will interfere with the magnetic pulses and an alarm will sound.

This device has been developed to detect faint traces of chemicals from explosives on a person's skin or clothes.

CANINES VERSUS CHEMICALS

Many airports have machines called chemical sniffers. These can detect tiny amounts of the substances used to make bombs. Security staff wipe the fingers of suspected bombers with a special cloth or pad. The chemical sniffer detects any trace of bomb-making chemicals and warns security staff of any possible risk.

So far, however, nothing can outperform the sniffer dog. These specially trained dogs sniff out the faint smells given off by bomb-making chemicals. If the dog smells something suspicious, it will bark and immediately direct its handler to the package or person.

SURVEILLANCE

Surveillance means **monitoring** (keeping track of) someone's activities and gathering information about them. Usually this is done without the person knowing about it. Governments and law enforcement agencies use surveillance to give them warnings about possible crimes or terrorist attacks.

CCTV

Closed-circuit television (CCTV) is a very common type of surveillance used in many countries. Video cameras are set up in public places, such as town centres. The images may be monitored on screens in police control centres or by local government officers. Shops may have their own cameras, monitored by their own staff.

PRIVACY ISSUES

Britain is said to have more CCTV cameras per person than any other country. No one knows exactly how many there are. Some people think there may be over four million cameras. This has led many people to worry about their privacy being invaded. Even though they are doing normal, innocent things, they are still being recorded.

CCTV cameras like these monitor activities in towns and cities all over the United Kingdom.

Smart cameras

The town of East Orange in New Jersey, USA, has been leading the way in monitoring and responding to crime. It is using "smart cameras" that can identify when crimes are taking place. They allow police to respond to an incident very quickly.

The smart cameras can be programmed to recognise the way people behave. For example, if a camera spots one person seeming to threaten another it issues an alert. An officer at the police department can zoom in on the computer to see if a crime is actually taking place. Meanwhile another computer program sends the information to a laptop in the police patrol car nearest to the scene. The time from alert to response may be only seconds.

Critics of the cameras point out that it can often be easy for the computer to mistake an innocent act for a criminal one. However, according to the police there, violent crime in East Orange has fallen by more than two-thirds since the smart cameras were introduced.

A CCTV camera has captured the moment a thief steals a woman's handbag.

11:23:20

11:23:25

11:23:30

11:23:31

11:23:32

11:23:33

Facial recognition

If the police are searching for someone in a crowd or on a busy street, they need to be able to pick out the person they are looking for from everyone else. One of the things that help us to tell people apart is that we all have different facial features. Generally speaking, we each have two eyes, a nose, a mouth, and so on. But facial features are all different shapes and distances apart. <u>Facial recognition software breaks up a face's features into measurements called **nodal points**</u>. These can be used to identify someone.

Police forces take photos of the people they arrest. This means they have a huge database of faces for comparison. Features such as hairstyle or facial hair are ignored as these can easily be changed. The distance between the eyes, for example, cannot.

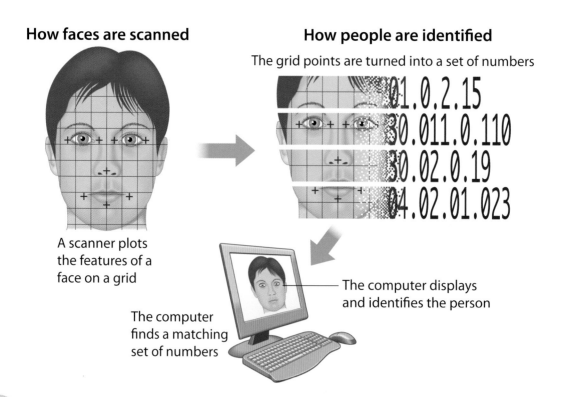

How faces are scanned

A scanner plots the features of a face on a grid

How people are identified

The grid points are turned into a set of numbers

01.0.2.15
30.011.0.110
30.02.0.19
04.02.01.023

The computer finds a matching set of numbers

The computer displays and identifies the person

Image capture

What makes facial recognition different from other forms of identification is that it can be done without any physical contact taking place. An image of a person's face can be captured on camera from a distance without their knowledge.

The captured image can then be analysed by a computer. It looks at the nodal points on the image and attempts to match them to other images held in police files.

A FACE IN THE CROWD

So far, facial recognition systems are not as good at picking out particular faces in a crowd as humans are. The software can compare millions of faces in a second – but it still needs a human to confirm that a match is accurate.

Face app

Police officers in the United States have been fighting crime using smartphones. The police officer can take a picture of a suspect using a facial recognition app (application). This uploads the picture to the police database for identification. If a match is made, the person's identity will appear on the officer's smartphone screen within seconds. Eye scanning and fingerprint recognition apps may also be added. This means that people can very quickly be identified with a high degree of certainty.

Listening in

Sometimes law enforcement agencies keep track of a person's activities by listening in to their conversations. There are various devices for doing this.

Bugging the line

Telephone tapping, or wire tapping, allows someone to intercept (listen in to) and record phone conversations. One of the simplest ways of listening in on a telephone is to place a tiny radio **transmitter** (device that sends out signals) inside the phone itself. This device is often called a "bug". The bug sends the telephone calls to a **receiver** hidden nearby. Another way is to attach wires to the telephone line outside. These can be connected to headphones and used to listen to the conversation.

Telephone companies can listen to any call being made. The police and security services can request that this be done if they have good reason to believe that monitoring a person's calls may prevent a crime.

Tapping into the telephone wires leading from the building allows a person to listen in to telephone conversations.

Wiretap headphones

Telephone

Wall socket

Power supply

Mobile phones

It is also possible to listen in to mobile phone conversations. Mobile phones work by transmitting **radio waves**. With the right equipment, these radio waves can be intercepted and listened to. As with landlines, police may also ask the mobile phone company's permission to allow them to listen to the calls being made from a particular phone.

Laser listening

It is even possible to listen in on a conversation using light. Sounds inside a room cause the glass in windows to vibrate slightly. An invisible **laser** beam can be pointed at the window from some distance away. A laser is like a very tightly focused beam of light. This beam is reflected back from the window to a laser receiver. The receiver detects the tiny vibrations in the window. It converts them into electronic signals which can be played through a speaker and recorded. It is possible to build both the transmitter and the receiver into something that looks just like an ordinary camera.

A laser listening device can detect tiny vibrations in a window caused by sounds in the room.

Lasers

Glass window

Recording device

Headphones

People in room

Signal converter

EYES IN THE SKY

One of the most effective pieces of surveillance equipment used by police forces is the helicopter. From high in the air, officers can use cameras and infrared sensors to track suspects.

A helicopter can cover large areas quickly. In 12 minutes, a helicopter can cover an area that would take 50 officers on the ground about 9 hours to search. It can be used to track criminals, search for a missing person, or find an abandoned vehicle. Police officers in the air can check places that are difficult for officers on the ground to reach, such as rooftops or fenced-off areas.

CAMERAS AND SENSORS

A video camera with a powerful zoom lens can be attached under the helicopter's nose. A special mount allows it to swivel in any direction. A high-powered searchlight mounted at the rear of the helicopter can be linked to the video camera. Its beam can be expanded to light up an area the size of a football pitch or reduced to pick out a single person running in the darkness.

searchlight

camera

Thermal imaging

A **thermal imager** may be placed alongside the camera. This detects the infrared radiation given off by a warm object, such as a hot car engine or a person hiding. The image is displayed on a screen inside the helicopter.

Downlinking

The helicopter crew can use microwave transmitters to send live video pictures to control centres and other police units on the ground. This is called downlinking. This view from the air is very useful in providing a "bird's eye" view of a crime scene.

The officers on board the helicopter can also communicate with people on the ground through a public address system. This can be used in crowd control or to warn people of danger, for example.

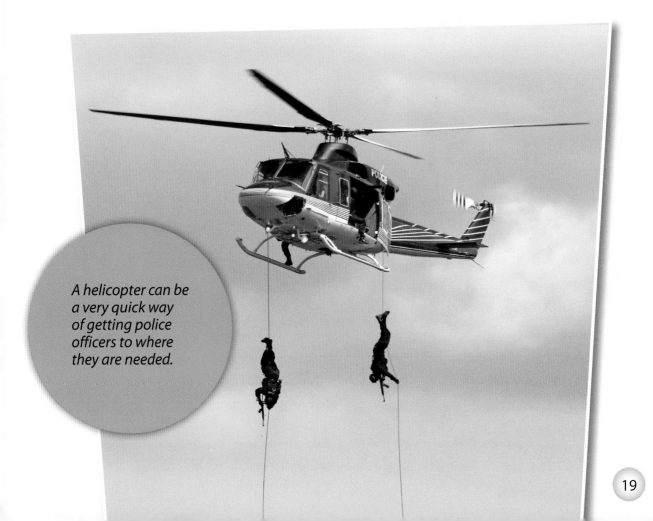

A helicopter can be a very quick way of getting police officers to where they are needed.

Spy planes

Police forces in Britain have been testing out unmanned aerial vehicles (UAVs). <u>UAVs are also known as spy drones (aircraft piloted by remote control)</u>. These spy drones are like the ones used for gathering intelligence (information) in war zones.

The British government hopes to have a fleet of drones in use when London hosts the Olympic Games in 2012. The "flying robot" fleet will range from small craft such as the miniature AirRobot, to the new, larger HERTI (High Endurance Rapid Technology Insertion) drone. The drones are much cheaper to build and operate than police helicopters and could take over many of their tasks.

An operator on the ground controls an AirRobot surveillance drone.

Bird's eye view

Smaller drones such as AirRobot will fly at about 1,000 metres (3,280 feet). The larger ones such HERTI will reach heights of around 6,000 metres (20,000 feet). This will make them invisible from the ground. An operator wearing a pair of video goggles guides AirRobot from the ground. The goggles are linked to the camera on the spy drone so the operator sees what the drone sees. The image from the drone can also be transmitted to a laptop screen. The HERTI drones are programmed to take off and land on their own and can stay airborne for up to 15 hours.

Voice from above

Unmanned aircraft can also be fitted with speakers, such as the Long Range Acoustic Device (LRAD). The LRAD is a speaker that can produce an intense beam of sound. Like the speakers on a crewed helicopter, it can be used as a loudhailer to send instructions to people on the ground. It can also produce a sudden burst of deafening noise that is loud enough to force people away. American police used LRAD mounted on ground vehicles to break up protestors at a meeting of world leaders in Pittsburgh, USA in 2009.

Strobe stopper

A spy drone could catch criminals too, rather than just making them flee. Powerful searchlights, like those on helicopters, could be adapted to turn into **strobe lights**. These intense, rapidly flashing lights can cause dizziness and loss of balance, stopping criminals in their tracks. This sort of light would be too dangerous to use in a crewed helicopter because of the risk of the crew being affected by it. That isn't a problem for a robot drone.

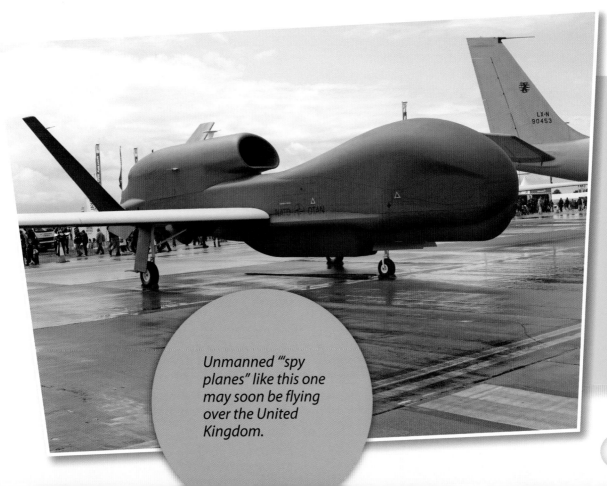

Unmanned "'spy planes" like this one may soon be flying over the United Kingdom.

Satellites and tracking

Police forces make good use of the Global Positioning System (GPS – see panel). It can be used to keep track of officers on foot patrol so they can be located (found) quickly. It is used to track the nearest police car to an emergency and get it there by the quickest route. Police can also track a stolen car using the GPS inside it.

GPS tracking

Vehicle tracking makes use of both GPS and the mobile phone system. The GPS pinpoints the vehicle's location. The phone system relays this information to a control centre. The GPS can be programmed to send an alert to the owner, or a security company, if an unauthorized person moves the vehicle.

WHAT IS GPS?

Twenty-four GPS satellites orbit Earth in space. Each one transmits a constant signal, which can be picked up by a GPS receiver. The receiver accurately calculates its distance from each of four different satellites, based on the time it takes for the signals to arrive. It then uses that information to work out its position on the surface of Earth.

GPS devices can be small enough to fit in a pocket.

BAIT BIKES

Police in Britain have been using GPS-equipped bikes to stop thieves. The bikes, which are deliberately poorly locked, are left in places where bike thefts happen often. Using the hidden GPS trackers, the police can trace the gangs behind the thefts. In Cambridge, where the bait bikes have been tried out, thefts from the railway station bike racks fell by nearly a half (50 per cent).

Tracker

Tracker is a device that helps police to find stolen vehicles. A transmitter is fitted into the car. It can be triggered remotely (from a distance) if the vehicle is reported as being stolen. It sends out radio signals that can be picked up by a police car or helicopter fitted with a special receiver. The radio signals can be picked up even if the car is hidden in an underground car park, for example. The stolen vehicle can quickly be identified through a unique code known only to the police.

GPS and mobile phone networks can be used together to track a stolen vehicle.

Satellite

2. Tracking device sends position via the mobile phone network

Tracking device

Mobile phone network

1. Tracking device uses GPS satellites to work out its position

3. Tracking control centre collects the vehicle's position

Stolen vehicle

THE SCENE OF THE CRIME

After a crime has been committed it isn't always obvious who did it or how it was done. Detectives use their skills and technology to discover what happened. Investigators will look for a number of clues, such as fingerprints, traces of blood, fibres from clothes, or marks made by tools. They will use these clues to piece together the puzzle and solve the crime.

SOCO/CSI

Scene of Crime Officers (**SOCO**s) in the United Kingdom, or Crime Scene Investigators (**CSI**s) in the United States, have an important role to play in fighting crime. It is their job to gather **evidence** from the crime scene. This can involve taking photographs of the scene before it is disturbed – the position of an object might be an important clue. They will look for fingerprints, traces of hair or fibres from clothes, and other signs that a criminal might have left behind.

These investigators are gathering evidence at a crime scene in Mexico City, Mexico.

Luminol

Luminol is a substance used by investigators to help find traces of blood. Crime investigators carefully spray luminol over an area where they suspect there may have been blood. If there is any blood, it causes a chemical reaction with the luminol that creates a blue glow. The amount of blood needed to trigger the reaction is very small. Luminol will even reveal where attempts have been made to remove bloodstains. The blue glow only lasts for about 30 seconds. But this is enough time for the investigators to take photographs which can be used as evidence.

Luminol has been used to reveal that the person whose footprint this is has stepped in blood.

If the shoe fits ...

Photographs of shoeprints or tyre tracks left at a crime scene can be transmitted from a crime scene straight on to a database. Here they will be analysed and matched up with thousands of other shoeprints and tracks. Shoeprints can help link someone to a crime scene. If a suspect is arrested, his shoes can be checked to see if they match the prints that have been found. Unlike a fingerprint, a shoeprint isn't conclusive evidence (proof without doubt), but it helps the detectives to build their case.

Everyone has a unique set of fingerprints that can be used to identify them.

Fingerprints

Searching for fingerprints at a crime scene is a tried and trusted method of identifying who has been present. <u>There are two types of fingerprint</u>. Visible prints are those left imprinted in a soft material, like a bloodstain or fresh paint. **Latent** prints are the ones that are made when oils on the skin are left behind after touching a surface. This makes a copy of the fingerprints. Latent prints are usually invisible to the naked eye.

Seeing fingerprints

The oldest – and still the most used – method of making latent prints visible is to dust the surface of an object with a powder. The powder sticks to the oils in the print so it can be seen. The investigator can then photograph the print or take a copy of it by carefully pressing sticky tape over the powder. Another way to look for prints is by using a laser beam. Latent prints will become visible when the light from a laser shines on them.

Database search

Once the fingerprints have been taken they can be compared against a database of fingerprints to see if there is a match. In the past this was done by eye and could take up to two weeks to carry out. Today, computer software can come up with a match in around 20 minutes.

Fingerprint scanners

Police can now use mobile phone-sized fingerprint scanners to check the identity of suspects instantly. The scanners can also be used to help identify murder **victims**. The index finger is scanned and the file is transmitted via computer or mobile phone to the central fingerprint database for checking.

BIOMETRICS

If you look closely at your fingertips you will see a pattern of lines. This pattern is different for everyone. Even identical twins have different prints. Your fingerprints stay the same throughout your life. This means that fingerprints can be used to identify a person. The study of the ways in which people differ from each other according to their body characteristics is called biometrics.

This is a mobile fingerprint scanner used by troops in Afghanistan. Police forces use similar models.

DNA profiling

There is a type of code that is found in all living things. That code is **DNA**. It carries the instructions for building and maintaining a new living thing. <u>DNA is passed on from one generation to the next and each person has a different DNA code from every other.</u> This means that everyone has a different DNA profile (set of information used for identification). Every part of the body contains this DNA profile. In theory, the smallest skin flake left behind at a crime scene can be used to determine (find) the DNA profile of a suspect.

Building a profile

A tiny amount of DNA from a drop of blood, a single hair, or a flake of skin from a fingerprint can be grown into a larger sample. This sample can be examined and used to create a profile.

This scientist is comparing DNA profiles in a laboratory.

DNA databases

Scientists can examine a DNA profile and compare it with a sample taken from a suspect or with the samples already held in a DNA database. The UK has the biggest DNA database in the world, with over three million profiles. If police scientists find a match they can be certain that there is less than a one in one billion chance that the samples came from different people. But if there is no match, the investigators can be sure that the person they suspected is innocent.

Contamination

The equipment used to create a DNA profile is very sensitive. Investigators have to take great care to make sure that samples are not contaminated (mixed with unwanted substances). If their own, or anyone else's DNA gets into a sample, the results are worthless. Full protective clothing, including facemasks, is worn when the sample is being taken from the crime scene. It is also worn when the sample is being examined in the laboratory.

CRIME AND COMPUTERS

As more and more of our activities take place on the Internet so it becomes a target for criminals. Police forces cannot do much to trace those who use computers to carry out crimes. Often the police will find that the criminals are based in other countries. This makes it difficult to bring them to justice.

International crime

Because the Internet spans the world, it means that criminals using it can operate on an international basis. It is possible for criminals in one country to gain access to people's bank accounts in another country.

Being vigilant

We all have to be sensible at protecting our personal details while online. Security software, **antivirus software**, and computer **firewalls** can all help to prevent an outsider getting access to and damaging a computer. These protections should all be kept up to date and made full use of.

Types of fraud

- 26%
- 18%
- 13%
- 9%
- 5%
- 12%
- 17%

Credit card fraud
Phone, heating, lighting, water bill fraud
Bank fraud
Job fraud
Loan fraud
Government document and benefits fraud
Other fraud

Piracy

One of the biggest computer crimes is that of piracy. This is the illegal copying, using, and selling of things such as music, DVDs, computer games, and software. There are many different ways to stop this from happening. For example, computer software comes with a unique code key that must be entered before the software can be used.

Skimming

Skimming is when identity thieves try and get the details of a person's bank card. One way of doing this is to fit a false panel on to a bank **ATM** (cash point machine). A tiny camera hidden inside the ATM records the personal identification number (PIN) entered by the card owner. At the same time, a device called a skimmer reads the magnetic strip on the back of the card. If thieves get hold of this information, they can make a copy of the card and use it to take out cash or buy goods.

The police have created an anti-skimming device. It is placed invisibly behind the ATM screen beside the real card reader. If it detects a skimmer in operation, it can prevent it from working. It can also detect illegal devices, such as cameras, attached to the ATM.

*Card readers like this one are meant to help prevent **fraud** (dishonesty) but criminals may still target them.*

Future crime

The police can use the powerful database and analysis tools of the computer to combat crime. In 2010, UK and US police forces even began trying to predict crimes before they happened.

Predictive analytics

Using powerful computer software, police information technology experts combined lots of information. This included past crimes, known behaviour patterns of offenders, surveillance information, reports of crimes, and even the weather. The software uses all of this data to predict where crimes are most likely to take place.

The science that allows these predictions to be made is called **predictive analytics**. The IBM computer company has developed the software. When it was tested in Memphis, Tennessee, USA, crime rates fell by nearly one-third. In Florida, the US Department of Justice used the software to predict which young offenders (criminals under the age of 18) were most likely to go on to become adult criminals.

This crime might be included in the information used to predict whether the offender will commit crimes in the future.

Repeat offenders

In Britain, the Ministry of Justice used predictive analytics to pinpoint which prisoners were likely to commit further crimes when they were released. Various factors such as education, lifestyle, family relationships, and drug use were all taken into account. The idea was that people picked out by the computer as likely offenders could be given the help they needed to avoid crime in the future.

BRIGHT IDEA?

Professor Richard Berk of the University of Pennsylvania developed predictive analytics software. It takes more than 20 different factors into account in making its predictions. In some cases, these predictions have proved to be very accurate.

However, some people are worried about predictive analytics. They say that it means people could be judged for something that they haven't actually done – just something they might do. If the results are wrong, it could mean someone being accused for just thinking about committing a crime!

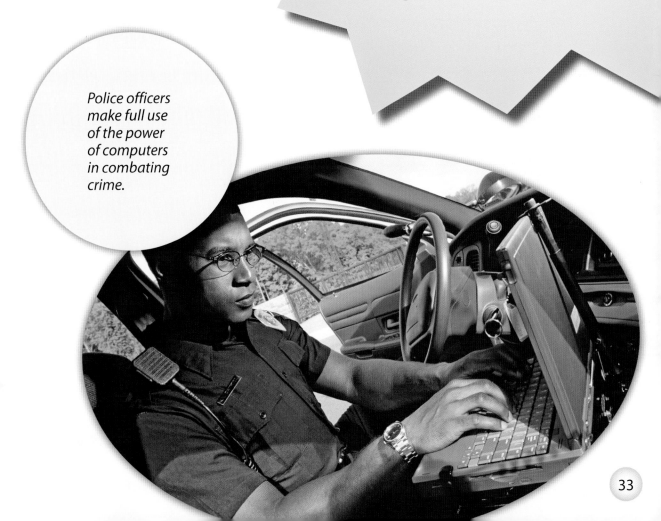

Police officers make full use of the power of computers in combating crime.

DEALING WITH DANGER

One of the most dangerous jobs in the fight against crime and terrorism is dealing with explosive devices such as bombs. Highly trained squads carry out this work. These squads can be made up of police officers or members of the armed forces.

Remote control

How experts set about tackling a bomb will depend on a number of things, such as the type of device and its position. If possible, the bomb disposal team will try to deal with the bomb from a distance. They have a number of long-range devices to help them in their work.

The Wheelbarrow

The bomb disposal team may use a device called the Wheelbarrow. It is controlled remotely, which means that the operator can send it into a dangerous situation without too much risk to himself.

Remote-controlled devices like this allow bomb disposal experts to examine bombs as safely as possible.

Getting around

The Wheelbarrow runs on a caterpillar track, like the ones found on bulldozers and tanks. It allows the Wheelbarrow to move easily over rough ground. The Wheelbarrow can even climb up stairs on its track. It has an extendible arm that can rotate full circle. The arm can be fitted with equipment such as cameras and chemical sensors. The operator uses these to build up a picture of the bomb.

Hands-on heroes

When a bomb cannot be dealt with remotely, a bomb technician must approach it directly. He puts on a heavily **armoured** protection suit made of a material similar to that used in bulletproof vests. The suit protects all parts of the body, but this restricts movement. It also cuts down on how easily the technician can see around him. So while offering protection, it also makes the technician's job a little harder.

Bomb suits contain cooling systems so the technician doesn't overheat inside the heavy suit. They also have built-in radio communications. These allow the technician to report on his progress in making the bomb safe.

A bomb technician wears full protective gear.

Staying safe

Sometimes police officers may find themselves in dangerous situations. In those circumstances there are various items of protective clothing and other equipment they can use to help reduce the risk of injury.

Riot shields

Police riot shields give protection from objects thrown during large-scale disturbances. They are made of strong, clear plastic, and come in a variety of sizes. They range from full body length to smaller, round shields.

Shields and visors protect officers in crowd control situations.

Stab vests

Being attacked by someone armed with a knife is one of the hazards a police officer may face. Wearing a stab vest gives some protection. The stab vest has a very tightly woven fabric made of heavy nylon. It takes a great deal of force to push a knife through it. It means that the officer is much less likely to be seriously injured.

Bulletproof vest

A bulletproof vest is designed to protect the wearer from gunshot wounds. There are two types: soft vests and rigid vests. Like stab vests, soft vests are made of a tightly woven fabric. This fabric is made of a very strong, but flexible, material called **Kevlar**. It allows the wearer to move around normally and spreads the force of a bullet's impact across the tight weave of the vest. This means there is not enough force left for the bullet to seriously injure the officer. Soft vests are effective against handguns. However, they may not stop a high-powered rifle bullet, which travels faster than that from a handgun.

Body armour

Rigid vests are like the armour worn by knights in the past. Instead of being made of metal, however, they are made of a tough, light material. Bullets simply bounce off a rigid vest. But it is not so easy to move around while wearing one. A bulletproof vest doesn't prevent all injury. The bullet might not penetrate (pierce) the skin, but the force of impact will still leave severe and painful bruising.

A stab vest like this protects a police officer from knife attack.

Fighting back

Police officers need some means of fighting back as well as defending themselves. Although weapons such as handguns may be used in extreme circumstances, there are other options that are less deadly.

For example, there are shotguns that can fire non-deadly **ammunition** such as the bean-bag round. The "bean bag" is a small fabric sack filled with small balls of lead. When it is fired from the shotgun, the sack spreads out as it flies through the air. It delivers a heavy blow on impact. It is a short-range weapon, and is accurate up to 12 metres (40 feet).

Flash-Ball

Special units of the French police force use the Flash-Ball gun. It looks like a large double-barrelled handgun. It can be used to fire a variety of ammunition, such as **tear gas** or a soft rubber ball. It is possible to have different types of ammunition in each barrel. According to the manufacturers of the Flash-Ball, being struck by the rubber ball is like being punched by a professional boxer!

A French police officer gets ready to fire a tear gas gun at rioters.

Water cannon

One very effective way of breaking up a crowd of rioters is to use a water cannon. The water cannon is mounted on a truck and can shoot a high-pressure jet of water a distance of 40 to 60 metres (140 to 200 feet). The truck holds about 8,000 litres (1,800 gallons) of water and the operator can safely direct the cannon from inside the truck.

Electroshock

Electroshock weapons work by giving an electric shock that can stun a person. The shock also makes them lose control of their muscles for a short time. The Taser is one such weapon. It fires two darts, which stay connected to the gun by long, thin wires. The darts and wires are held in a case called a cartridge. The cartridge is replaced after each use. The main body of the gun holds the batteries that send the electric charge through the wires. It has a maximum range of around 10 metres (35 feet).

The Taser delivers a high-voltage electric shock.

FUTURE TECHNOLOGY

Some researchers imagine a time when much police work will be carried out by robots. How close is this to becoming a reality? Police in the United States recently borrowed a special robot from NASA, the United States' space agency, to help them in a hunt for evidence to a crime. The following story shows how it was used.

Buried evidence

In 1991, Dawn Sanchez was killed. The gun used to kill her, and the car in which she was last seen, could not be found. Due to this important lack of evidence, the man suspected of the crime could not be charged with her murder.

Almost 20 years later, someone informed the police that the car had been taken apart and buried in a large area of wasteground in Alviso, California. The problem was that the exact location of the car was unknown. Also, there were far too many other pieces of junk metal buried there to make a search with metal detectors possible.

Calling NASA

The police turned for help to the experts at the United States Geological Survey (USGS), who in turn called on the scientists at NASA. They had been working on magnetic and ground-penetrating radar sensors. Ground-penetrating radar uses microwaves to "see" beneath the ground. Under ideal conditions it can reveal things up to 15 metres (50 feet) below the surface. NASA uses sensors like this mounted on small air and ground robots as part of their Earth Science investigations.

Together, a team of computer software experts and scientists from NASA and USGS took a robot equipped with sensors to the wasteground.

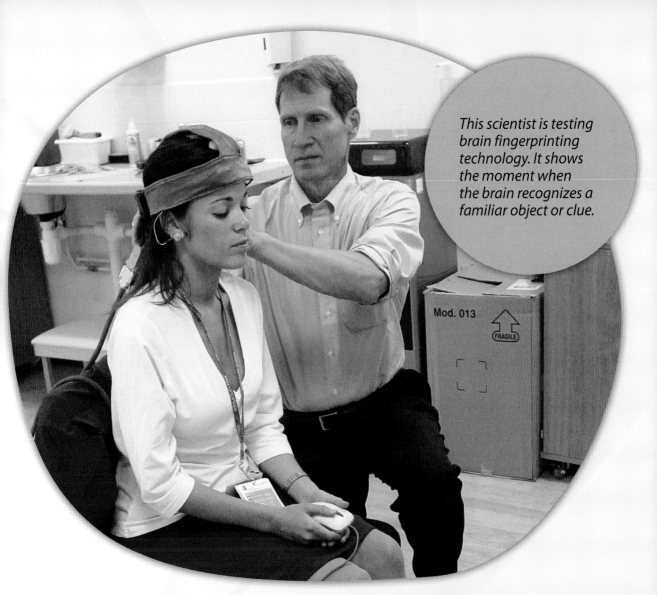

This scientist is testing brain fingerprinting technology. It shows the moment when the brain recognizes a familiar object or clue.

Robot justice

The rover used its sensors to survey the area. The map it built up was analysed by the software experts. They were able to pinpoint the most likely locations for the buried car. Following the experts' recommendations, the police began to dig. They found car parts that did indeed match the suspect's car.

Faced with this evidence in court in August 2009, Bernardo Bass was found guilty of the **manslaughter** of Dawn Sanchez. This was 18 years after the crime was committed. Once again, advanced technology had come to the aid of the police.

TIMELINE

3000 BC
One of the earliest police forces was created in Egypt. The pharaoh (Egyptian ruler) gave several people the job of providing justice (fairness) and security in the country. The chief of police for each district had the title *sab heri seker*, which means "chief of the hitters".

7 BC
Policing used to be looked on as a very low-ranking job. The ancient Greeks and Romans used slaves, and even some former criminals, as police. In 7 BC the emperor Augustus created an organized police force in Rome. It was also responsible for dealing with fires.

5th–11th centuries
In Anglo-Saxon England, before the Norman conquest of 1066, all adult males were responsible for each other's good behaviour. If a crime was seen to take place, everyone was expected to raise an alarm, called a "hue and cry", and chase after the criminal. Areas of the country, called shires, were led by a shire-reeve. This is where the modern word *sheriff* comes from.

1066
When the Normans conquered England, they introduced the office of constable, a name still used for a police officer. Originally, constables worked in the royal court. Later they took on other tasks, such as guarding the city gates, dealing with violent crimes, and watching out for fires.

1750
Brothers Henry and John Fielding set up an organization known as the Bow Street Runners. They paid their constables (*see* "1066") to patrol the area around Bow Street in London.

1829
The London Metropolitan Police Department came into being. People did not want the police to be like the army, which was controlled by politicians and wore red uniforms. So constables and officers were given blue uniforms and did not carry guns. The Metropolitan Police became a model for police forces across Britain, the United States, and elsewhere in the world.

1842
The Metropolitan Police set up its first detective branch. This later became the Criminal Investigations Department (CID). Police departments in US cities soon had detectives, too.

1923
Interpol was founded by the police chief of Vienna, Austria. Today, over 180 member countries share information about criminal activities. They help each other out with investigations and arrests.

1865
The US Secret Service was set up to combat counterfeiting – the illegal printing of banknotes. Since 1901 they have had the role of guarding the president of the United States, too.

1798
The Thames River Police were set up in London to combat crime in what was then the world's largest port. They mounted patrols along the river and were a big success.

1908
The Federal Bureau of Investigation (FBI) was formed in the United States. Its job is to enforce criminal laws and protect the country from terrorist attacks.

Glossary

ammunition things fired from a gun, such as bullets or shells

antivirus software software designed to prevent harmful viruses from working on a computer

armoured covered by armour, a hard covering designed to protect from attack

ATM (automated teller machine) type of computer usually found beside a bank. It allows a person to take money from their account.

CSI (Crime Scene Investigator) in the United States, the name given to a police officer who looks for evidence at the scene of a crime

database collection of information gathered together so that different items can be easily sorted and found

DNA large molecule found in the cells that make up all living things; it carries the information needed for making and maintaining an organism

electric circuit path for electricity to flow through

electromagnet type of magnet that works when electricity flows through a coil of wire

evidence something used to prove that something has happened. Fingerprints at a crime scene are evidence that someone was there.

firewall type of software protection for computers that stops other people getting access to the computer on a network

fraud deliberately deceiving someone in order to gain an unlawful benefit

identify establish the identity of a person, to recognize them

infrared "colour" beyond red in the spectrum; it is invisible to our eyes but we can feel it as heat

intruder someone who enters a home or building without permission

Kevlar type of very strong yet light fibre; it is five times stronger than steel but very flexible

laser high energy, tightly focused beam of light

latent something which is there but cannot be seen at the moment; a latent fingerprint has to be treated with powder to make it visible, for example

law enforcement agency branch of government whose job it is to see that the laws of the land are obeyed; the police are one law enforcement agency

manslaughter kill someone without meaning to

microwave short type of energy wave that can be used to send information

monitor to watch, keep track of, or check

nodal point distinguishing feature of the face, such as the distance between the nostrils or the width of the eyes

predictive analytics way of analyzing information and using it to try to predict the future

property personal belongings

radio wave energy wave that can send signals through the air without using wires

receiver something for detecting energy waves such as microwaves or radio waves sent by a transmitter

satellite object that travels around a larger object in space, such as a weather satellite going around Earth

security services government institutions which provide secret intelligence, such as MI5 and MI6 in the UK

sensor something that detects something, such as light or sound

SOCO (Scene of Crime Officer) in the UK; someone who gathers evidence at the scene of a crime

strobe light device which produces a very bright flashing light

surveillance keeping a close watch on someone

tear gas gas that causes a burning sensation in the eyes, often used to control crowds

terrorist someone who uses violence and threats to achieve their aims

thermal imager device that detects heat and displays it visually on a screen

transmitter something that sends a signal, usually in the form of radio or other energy waves

victim person who comes to harm as the result of criminal activities

Find out more

Books

Crime Fighting, Nathaniel Harris (Gareth Stevens Publishing, 2009)

Crime Fighting (The Impact of Science and Technology), Anne Rooney (Franklin Watts, 2009)

Fighting Crime (Why Science Matters), Ian Graham (Heinemann Library, 2008)

Fingerprint Wizards, Steve Parker (A&C Black, 2009)

Solving Crimes in the Lab, Carol Ballard (Franklin Watts, 2010)

Solving Crimes with Trace Evidence, Gary Jeffrey (Franklin Watts, 2009)

Scene of the Crime, Malcolm Rose (Kingfisher Books, 2008)

Virtual Crime: Solving Cybercrime, Leon Gray (Enslow Publishers, 2009)

Websites

www.fbi.gov/fbikids.htm
The Federal Bureau of Investigation's Kids' page contains games and stories to help young people learn about the work of the FBI.

www.dnai.org/d/index.html
Learn more about DNA profiling.

news.bbc.co.uk/hi/english/static/in_depth/uk/2001/life_of_crime/cybercrime.stm
Information about cybercrime and how to combat it.

www.police.vic.gov.au/content.asp?Document_ID=12260
This is a fun introduction to the work of the police in Victoria, Australia.

www.centredessciencesdemontreal.com/static/autopsy/flash.htm
Help the Montreal police solve a murder in this animated crime scene.

www.mcgruff.org
This gives advice on staying safe and preventing crime from McGruff the Crimefighting Dog (a National Crime Prevention Council website).

www.army.mod.uk/rlc/regiments/8731.aspx
This is the website of the 11 EOD regiment of the British Army, specialists in dealing with explosive devices.

Topics to research

Computer security
Do you have personal information on a computer? What are the best ways to ensure that this is kept safe?

Shed some ultraviolet light on the subject
Find out whether security marker pens are available in your local shops. They contain ink that is only visible under ultraviolet light. Think about any items you might want to mark so that they could be identified as yours if they were stolen.

Thinkuknow
The Child Exploitation and Online Protection website has "thinkuknow" pages where you can find the latest safety information on the sites you like to visit, mobiles, and new technology. Find out what's good, what's not, and what you can do about it at www.thinkuknow.co.uk.

Is Big Brother watching you or looking after you?
Does the presence of a CCTV camera make you feel safe or does it suggest that you are in a high crime area?

Predictive analytics
Check out the arguments for and against predictive analytics. What are your own conclusions about using it as a way to reduce crime?

Index